HOW IT HAPPENED

SKATEBOARDS

The Cool Stories and Facts

Behind Every Trick

HOW iT HAPPENED

SKATEBOARDS

The Cool Stories and Facts

Behind Every Trick

BY PAIGE TOWLER

ILLUSTRATED BY DAN SIPPLE

union
square
kids

NEW YORK

union square kids

NEW YORK

UNION SQUARE KIDS and the distinctive Union Square Kids logo
are trademarks of Union Square & Co., LLC.

Union Square & Co., LLC, is a subsidiary of Sterling Publishing Co., Inc.

Copyright © 2024 WonderLab Group, LLC

ISBN 978-1-4549-4502-4 (hardcover)
ISBN 978-1-4549-4515-4 (paperback)
ISBN 978-1-4549-4503-1 (e-book)

Library of Congress Control Number: 2023031733

For information about custom editions, special sales, and premium purchases,
please contact specialsales@unionsquareandco.com.

Printed in Malaysia

Lot #:
2 4 6 8 10 9 7 5 3 1

11/23
unionsquareandco.com

Cover design by Liam Donnelly
Cover art by Becca Clason
Interior illustrations and series logo by Dan Sipple
Interior design by Nicole Lazarus
Created and produced by WonderLab Group, LLC
Photo research by Nicole DiMella
Sensitivity review by Nina Tsang
Factchecked by Debra Bodner and Kale Kanaeholo
Copyedited by Molly Reid
Indexed by Connie Binder
Proofread by Susan K. Hom
Image credits—see page 192

RAD!

TO A GREAT TEAM:
TOM, GAIL, AND BOB.
—P.T.

Table of Contents

Grab Your Boards

Quick: What is it that makes skateboards so cool? Is it the simple design that lets the pros land impossible-seeming jumps? Or is it the feeling of freedom you get while riding one?

Maybe you think the best parts of skateboarding don't even have to do with skateboards—after all, an entire culture has developed around skateboarding. In fact, you don't have to ride a skateboard to take part in skateboarding culture. From fashion to music to video games to art, skateboards have influenced people across the world.

But the story of the skateboard is about more than fashion and art. It's a story that spans thousands of years, journeying all the way from surfing in the ancient cultures of the Pacific Islands to the rise of celebrity skaters and into the Olympics—and the future.

SECTION ONE

How
It All
Started

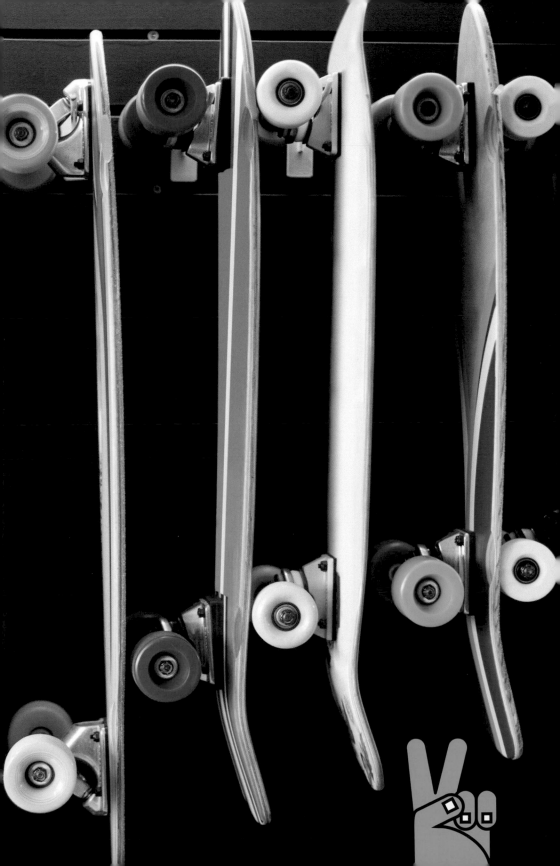

CHAPTER ONE

Surf's Up!

Early Innovators

When you think of skateboarding, what comes to mind? Amazing tricks? Customized skateboards? For millions of people around the world, skateboarding is a sport famed for its innovation and creativity, from the gear to the moves to the origin of the sport itself. The innovation that makes skateboarding fantastic and fresh has been happening for many years. In fact, it's been going on for thousands of years before skateboarding even existed.

To understand how and why skaters first hit the pavement, we need to journey all the way back to when people began hitting the *surf*. That's right—the first boards weren't skateboards, but surfboards.

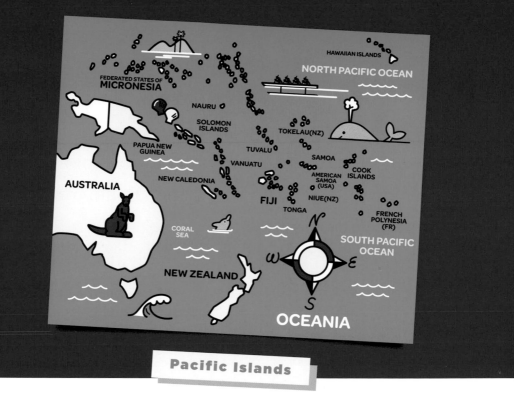

If you're looking to thank those responsible for skateboarding, you'll need to travel back in time to meet some of the first people to truly navigate, understand, and conquer the ocean: Some archaeologists today call this ancient culture the Lapita.

Around 40,000 years ago, modern humans began to explore the large islands of Southeast Asia using simple rafts. But by 1500 BCE, the Lapita wanted to explore farther. Building on the seafaring technology

created by their ancestors, the Lapita created sophisticated canoes and set out to explore a region of islands in the Pacific Ocean, today known as Oceania.

The Lapita were expert navigators who were able to find their way across long ocean distances without relying on the modern tools sailors use today. Sometimes called **wayfinders**, these navigators memorized the positions of hundreds of stars. They also knew how to observe changes in the weather, the clouds, and even the waves to determine whether land might be nearby.

Scientists aren't sure why the Lapita first started exploring the seas. It's possible that they were looking for new lands as they were vulnerable in their current homes to a disease called malaria, which is carried by mosquitoes.

Outrigger canoes were used by early explorers in the Pacific.

They may have been experiencing a **drought**. Another possibility is that they may have just been curious and eager to explore.

Over hundreds of years, the Lapita ventured far into the Pacific and settled many islands in the region known today as the Pacific Islands. These journeys were long and dangerous. To navigate the seas, Lapita explorers needed to understand and rely on the ocean. Over time, thanks to their expert knowledge of the water, these Lapita settlements grew into different ocean-based societies, that today some collectively refer to as Pacific cultures.

Māori people participate in a traditional dance at a street festival.

Pacific Cultures

There is no "one" Pacific culture—there are many. Over time, groups of people living in different parts of the Pacific developed separate languages, customs, and religions. These grew into many distinct cultures and nationalities today, such as the Māori in New Zealand, the Hawaiians of the Hawaiian Islands, the Tahitians of French Polynesia, and many more. However, different Pacific cultures often share similarities, some of which may even have been preserved from Lapita culture. In fact, historians believe that several designs used in traditional Pacific tattoos come from the distinct art the Lapita often used to decorate their pottery.

So, what does the settling of the Pacific have to do with skateboarding? Simple: the Pacific was soon to become the home of a surfing culture that would not only travel the world but also give rise to skateboarding thousands of years later.

"There is not one right way to ride a wave."

—JAMIE O'BRIEN, PROFESSIONAL SURFER

There are more than a thousand islands that make up the Pacific.

Ancient Boards

Petroglyph from Hawai'i

So, if skateboarding got its start from surfing, how exactly did surfing take off?

Across the Pacific Islands, the scene was set: Early innovators had learned to navigate the ocean and relied on it for survival. It was only a matter of time before they turned to the sea for sport, too!

Scientists aren't sure when or where Pacific Islanders first broke out the boards. However, rock carvings, or petroglyphs, found in what is now Tonga show what appears to be a human figure on a triangular surfboard. This likely means that surfing has existed in the region since the 1400s. Experts have also discovered similar petroglyphs in Hawai'i that date back to the 1600s.

However, there are other historians who think that Pacific surfing might be even older: thousands of years old, in fact. Regardless of exactly when they first began, Pacific Islanders have been practicing the sport for centuries.

The earliest Pacific Islanders' surfboards were likely made from wood and were probably very large. This would have been necessary to keep the boards—and the people on them—floating. Surfboards depend on **buoyancy**. This is the upward force that a fluid, such as water, pushes onto an object. The more buoyant something is, the more easily it floats. Wood is naturally buoyant. However, this means that the big wooden surfboards were also probably very heavy to carry around.

"We're all equal before a wave."

—LAIRD HAMILTON, PROFESSIONAL SURFER

Pro surfer Bethany Hamilton surfs in a competition in Haleiwa, Hawai'i.

Surfing Science

In addition to balance, surfing also relies on **hydrodynamics**—the forces of moving water. When a surfer catches a wave, they must position their board at an angle to the wave. This creates pressure—or force—and causes the fluid of the wave to push back against the pressure, keeping the surfer on top of the water. Now the movement of the wave carries the surfer forward . . . as long as they keep their balance, that is!

On top of being strong enough to handle their boards, these surfers also had to balance two forces: buoyancy and **gravity**. While buoyancy pushes up on a board, gravity, the force of the Earth's pull, pulls downward. All surfers—from early Pacific Islanders to surfers today—have to keep these forces in balance to make sure their boards skim along the top of the water. Otherwise, it's *splash!* into the sea.

The Bishop Museum in Hawai'i has a surfboard that's more than 230 years old.

> **"Arise, arise, ye great surfs from Kahiki. The powerful curling waves."**
>
> —TRANSLATION OF A HAWAIIAN SURF CHANT

Despite the difficulties of this new sport, many Pacific Islanders became experts, just as they mastered ocean exploration. In fact, people of all ages, social ranks, and genders surfed. And in certain parts of the Pacific, surfing became more than a sport. It became an important part of the culture which, over many years, would indirectly lead to skateboarding.

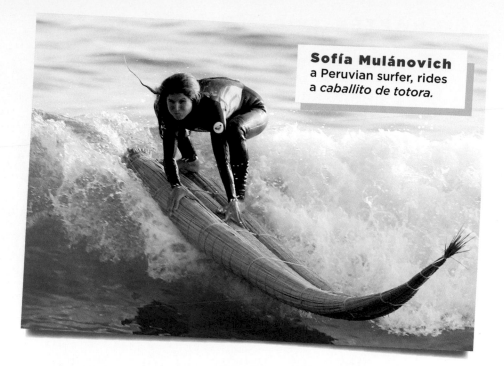

Sofía Mulánovich a Peruvian surfer, rides a *caballito de totora.*

Who Was the First?

The surfing culture that would soon spread across parts of the world—and eventually lead to the invention of skateboarding—originated in the Pacific. However, were Pacific Islanders the first people in the world to surf? Not necessarily. Some historians believe that people may have surfed in what is now known as Peru more than four thousand years ago—long before the Pacific was even settled. That's because today, many people surf in Peru using *caballitos de totora*, small boats made of bound reeds. These boats have ancient origins, and experts believe that people in the region may have been surfing this same way for thousands of years.

CHAPTER TWO
From Sea to Sidewalk

Troubled Waters

If surfing culture as we know it originated in the islands of the Pacific, how did it expand to the rest of the world? The truth is that it almost didn't.

For much of human history, Pacific Islanders and Europeans did not interact. As skilled sailors, explorers from the Pacific Islands traded with each other. Though scientists think these explorers may have reached as far as South America and even parts of Africa, much of the Pacific Islands—Hawai'i in particular—remained unknown to Europeans. But this was all about to change.

In 1778, British explorer James Cook arrived at the Hawaiian island of Kaua'i. Although Cook's aim was to explore, his

Scientists think that Pacific Islanders and Indigenous peoples in South America met as many as eight hundred years ago.

arrival had horrible consequences for the Indigenous population. Cook and his crew brought diseases that Native Hawaiians had never encountered. Because of this, they had no immunity, and many people died. Although Cook died a year later, his voyage meant that other Europeans now knew of Hawai'i's existence.

In the early 1800s, Christian missionaries began to arrive in Hawai'i. These Europeans intended to convert Native Hawaiians to Christianity. They were often ignorant of native customs and held many racist and prejudiced beliefs. They quickly began to take over the islands, banning many Hawaiian traditions and cultural practices. According to some scholars, missionaries also banned

How Hawaiʻi Became a State

For many centuries, the islands of Hawaiʻi were governed by different local rulers. In 1810, King Kamehameha I united the islands into one kingdom. However, as European and American missionaries and plantation owners flooded the islands, they began to seize control. In a plot led by the colonizers and parts of the U.S. government, a group of Americans violently overthrew Hawaiʻi's ruler Queen Liliʻuokalani in 1893. In 1898, the United States officially claimed Hawaiʻi as a **territory**. In 1959, after a vote among American citizens, Hawaiʻi became the nation's fiftieth state.

*"A fond embrace,
A hoʻi aʻe au
(Ere I depart),
Until we meet
again."*

**—LYRICS FROM "ALOHA ʻOE,"
WRITTEN BY QUEEN
LILIʻUOKALANI IN 1878**

surfing. However, other historians believe that it was not missionaries who prevented surfing, but another group of newly arrived colonizers: American plantation owners.

American business owners had begun to flock to Hawaiʻi. There, they established sugar plantations and forced local people to work the fields. Because of this, Native Hawaiians no longer had the time or freedom to surf. By the end of the century, surfing was in decline.

Saving Surfing

At the start of the twentieth century, Hawaiians were facing a takeover by the American government, oppression, and a completely new way of life. Surfing was not practiced on a scale even close to what it had been before. However, thanks to several extremely talented Hawaiian surfers, that was about to change.

In the late 1800s, Hawaiian princess Ka'iulani was a passionate activist who spoke out against her kingdom's colonization and annexation. She was also an incredibly talented surfer. As Princess Ka'iulani traveled the world, she spoke to world leaders such as U.S. president Grover Cleveland to advocate for Hawai'i's right to rule

Princess Ka'iulani

itself. In the process, she also dazzled people with her masterful surfing skills, even surfing the English Channel off the coast of England.

Similarly, in 1885, three Hawaiian princes, Jonah Kūhiō Kalaniana'ole, David Kawānanakoa, and Edward Keli'iahonui, traveled to California to study at a local university. There, they spent time surfing— and were perhaps among the first people to ever surf in the continental United States. Californians were so impressed by the sport that it was documented by local newspapers.

However, one of the most iconic surfers of the time was Duke Kahanamoku. Born in Hawaiʻi in 1890, Kahanamoku went on to represent the United States in the Olympics, winning three gold medals for swimming. Though he was considered one of the best swimmers on the planet, Kahanamoku's true passion was surfing. As he rose to fame as a swimmer, he also became famous for his beloved hobby and brought surfing onto the world's radar.

Along with the skills of these amazing athletes, increased tourism to Hawaiʻi was bringing more attention to the sport. Famous American author Jack London often visited the islands, and his writings on Hawaiian surfers such as George Freeth, the "father of modern surfing," ensured that readers across the planet now knew of the sport.

Aloha, Hawai'i

Tourism also helped popularize surfing in the late 1800s. Since then, tourism in Hawai'i has only increased—in fact, more than ten million people visited the state in 2019. That's nearly ten times as many people that live there! With Hawai'i's rich culture and stunning natural beauty, it is easy to see why people want to visit. However, the high number of tourists has also led to many problems, such as overcrowding, water shortages, and damage to the local environment. Many activists in Hawai'i are advocating for new approaches to tourism that would benefit locals and Native Hawaiians and help preserve their lands and water.

From Surfboard to Skateboard

Although surfing culture as we know it originated in the Pacific, it was now a cultural force around the world. It thrived in coastal places such as Southern California. In fact, it was so popular that many people wanted to surf all the time—even when the waves were flat or when they weren't near the water.

GNARLY!

Statue of Duke Kahanamoku

A man rides a *papa hōlua*, or land sled.

To solve this problem, enterprising surfers in the late 1940s and early 1950s created skateboards. At first, most people made skateboards at home by pulling the wheels off roller skates and attaching them to wooden boards and planks. So how did these early designs for skateboards come about?

According to historians, some people were inspired by the boards used in another Hawaiian sport: land sledding. A land sled, or *papa hōlua*, was a thin central platform attached to two long ski-like poles. Hawaiian

royalty, or *ali'i*, used these sleds to ride down grassy hills and even hardened lava. Riders may have slid down on their bellies, or balanced sideways on their feet, like surfers— and later, like skateboarders!

Other historians think that early skateboards may have been based on scooters. In the 1880s, bicycles had become wildly popular across the United States. Soon, companies were making children's toys inspired by these bicycles. These toys

Some of the first scooters were made from wooden planks.

featured a low platform with wheels and tall handlebars. They were called kick scooters and push scooters. Over the next few decades, it became popular for kids to remove the handlebars and just use their scooters almost like early versions of skateboards.

Early skaters were known as asphalt surfers.

Regardless of what early skateboards were based on, they were a hit with surfers and surfing culture. As more people began "sidewalk surfing," as it was known, some surf companies got in on the action, too, making and selling skateboards to surfers.

The skateboard had finally arrived. Now it had to break away from surfing and become a sport in its own right.

"Something new in surfboards!"

—1965 AD FOR THE "SPYDER" SIDEWALK SURFBOARDS

Snow Surfing

Around the time "sidewalk surfboards" were becoming popular in the United States, so was another surfing-like sport: snowboarding. Although snow sports and versions of snowboarding had existed around the world for centuries, its modern form took off in the 1960s thanks to an innovative father, Sherman Poppen. After a snowstorm, Poppen attempted to take his daughters sledding, but they were having trouble when the sled's blades got stuck. Instead, Poppen had an idea: Why not try to "surf" down the snowy hill? Poppen created an early version of the snowboard, which his wife, Nancy, named the snow surfer—or Snurfer. Over time, this design morphed into the snowboards we know today.

CHAPTER THREE

Ready to Roll

Ready, Set, Skate

When skateboarding rolled onto the scene around the 1950s, surfers could now practice some surfing skills on the street.

Like surfing, skateboarding relies a lot on balance. Surfers and skaters both usually use a side stance. This is a position where the rider faces sideways in a crouch with their legs spread evenly apart. A side stance lets riders keep their balance spread evenly over the board. It also lets them keep most of their weight (often referred to as the center of gravity) low to the board, making it less likely they will tip over.

Back in the 1950s, a surfer could practice their stance and their balance skills. They could also practice using their weight and

balance to turn the skateboard—just like on a surfboard. On top of that, crouching on a skateboard helped them strengthen their leg muscles, which helped make them stronger surfers.

However, there are also very important differences between surfing and skateboarding. Unlike with surfing, skateboarders couldn't rely on the motion of the water; they needed to create their own motion. To do this, most skateboarders use their rear foot to push along the ground while balancing on the board with their front foot. Once they have enough speed, their **momentum**, or moving weight, carries them forward.

Of course, this is also thanks to another big difference between skateboards and surfboards: the wheels. Invented more than five thousand years ago in what is now Iraq, wheels allow people to move heavy items—including themselves—by rolling them along the ground. A working wheel is made up of two main parts: the wheel itself and the **axle**. The axle is a type of pole that slips through the center of a wheel or through multiple wheels. This design lets the wheels keep moving around the axle. When attached to a board, wheels let people roll along.

Stop Right There!

Okay, so you've got your momentum going—but how do you stop a skateboard? The answer lies with **friction**. Friction is a force that occurs when one object slides or moves over another. This force acts against, or resists, movement. Friction is always there when a skateboard zooms along the ground. However, wheels let the skateboard overcome this friction to keep moving. But when a rider wants to slow down or stop, friction comes back into play. To stop, a skateboarder carefully drags their rear foot along the ground while remaining balanced on their front foot. This causes lots of friction, slowly bringing the skateboard to a stop.

As surfers began to get used to the differences between skateboards and surfboards, they soon realized something else: Skateboarding was fun! In fact, skateboarding was so much fun that people soon began skating for the fun of it, rather than to practice for surfing.

Skateboarding was far from the first wheeled sport: roller skates had been around since the 1700s.

Banned Boards

By the end of the 1950s, companies had caught on to the fact that skateboards were gaining popularity. However, most companies promoted the skateboard as an extension of surfing—or as a kid's toy.

But as more and more people became interested in skateboarding in the 1960s, they started to make the sport their own. Most people practiced skateboarding on flat ground. Surfers sometimes imitated the same types of moves that they used while on a surfboard. Others created choreography and added music, or even incorporated gymnastics. This came to be known as **freestyle** skating. Soon, companies dedicated to skateboards began to appear, such as Makaha and Hobie. These brands soon began to organize some of the first ever skateboarding competitions held in Southern California.

On top of that, skateboarding was gaining national attention in the United States. One professional skater named Patti McGee captivated fans across the country with her signature move: skateboarding while doing a handstand on her board, or **deck**. McGee brought the sport even more into the public view when she was photographed for the cover of *Life* magazine in May 1965. Soon, she was skating on famous television shows, too.

"There was a transition . . . from skateboards being toys to skateboards being equipment."

—PATTI MCGEE, PROFESSIONAL SKATEBOARDER

Patti McGee

By now, many people were interested in skating as its own sport—and not as an extension of surfing. People were eager to surf—or, as they now referred to it, skate—the streets. In fact, from 1963 to 1965, companies had made as many as fifty million skateboards. It seemed like skateboarding was sweeping the nation.

"[Skateboarding was] an epidemic from which no one was secure."

—*THE DEVIL'S TOY,* A 1966 CANADIAN FILM ON SKATEBOARDING

In Canada, skateboarding was first known as "skurfing."

A 1970s skater lands a hippy flip: a trick where a skater jumps off the skateboard and over an object, then lands back on the board on the other side.

However, it wasn't meant to be. Early skateboards were difficult to use and to move around. The boards' wheels were usually made of metal or clay and wore down or broke easily. Falls were common, and most people at the time didn't wear safety gear. Unlike with surfing though, falling didn't mean a splash into the water— it meant a tumble onto the rough pavement. This meant that many people were getting injured. In fact, so many skateboarders were being hurt that several American cities, such as Ocean City, Maryland, and Akron, Ohio, banned the sport completely. City officials even warned stores not to sell boards at all. It seemed like skateboarding might fade out.

How It Got Off the Ground

CHAPTER FOUR

Hitting the Streets

Streamlining the Skateboard

Hold on—skateboarding wasn't gone just yet. Things all began to change with new improvements. In the early 1960s, one surfer named Larry Stevenson had noticed kids riding around on homemade skateboards in his Southern California neighborhood. He also noticed that they weren't having the easiest time. He figured he could design a better version. At home in his garage, Stevenson began to design new "sidewalk surfboards" shaped after their namesakes. A more rounded, oblong shape made the board easier to steer. Pleased with his success, Stevenson went on to found the skateboard company Makaha.

Then, in 1969, Stevenson took things further when he invented the **kicktail**. This seemingly simple invention would go on to change the very nature of skateboarding. Previously, skateboards had generally been flat. Now the kicktail—the upward-curved end of the skateboard—made it possible to do **aerial** moves, or tricks in the air. Skaters could use the kicktail almost like a type of lever: By pushing down on the kicktail with their foot, a skater could send the board up into the air. Then, they could keep the board in the air with them by grabbing it before landing again. These types of tricks became known as grabs.

On top of that, other people were making improvements to skateboards as well. One big problem area was the wheels. Made of

clay or metal, these wheels did not stand up very well to friction and they wore down easily. In 1973, Frank Nasworthy, another innovative skater, used a material known as **polyurethane** to create special wheels for his skateboard. These new polyurethane wheels made the skateboard much easier to maneuver. They also were much sturdier and didn't tear apart on the pavement like other types of wheels. Nasworthy started his own company called Cadillac Wheels.

Polyurethane is also used in **spandex—** the **stretchy** **material** often found in **leggings.**

Deck

Nose

Anatomy of a Skateboard

A skateboard consists of three main parts: the deck, the trucks, and the wheels.

The main board is also known as the **deck**. Most decks are covered in **grip tape**, a sandpaper-like covering that helps riders grip the deck with their feet. The front of the deck is known as the **nose**, and the back is the **tail**. The curved ends of the deck are known as the kicktails.

Tail

Wheels

Trucks

The **trucks** of a skateboard are metal fixtures on the underside of the deck that connect the wheels to the deck. The trucks let a rider steer and bear the rider's weight, and they allow the rider to use their weight to turn the skateboard.

Today, most skateboard wheels are made from polyurethane. Skateboard wheels come in different sizes and shapes, and they can help the rider skate faster or perform different kinds of tricks.

Over the next few years, people began creating several new inventions that made the sport much safer. In 1975, bicycling companies began introducing helmets specially designed for cyclists. These helmets were light, unlike many sports helmets, and left the face area open so that riders could see all around themselves. However, they still protected a rider's head from falls: A hard outer shell helped spread the force of a crash over the whole helmet to lessen the blow; then, a thick layer of foam material on the inside of the helmet absorbed the force, keeping the rider's head safe. Soon, skateboarders were wearing these helmets, too—and skateboarding companies even began to create slightly different versions for skaters, designed to protect against multiple falls. (After all, it's a physical sport!)

Safety experts also came out with other types of protective gear, such as kneepads, wrist guards, and elbow pads. Like helmets, these all used a combination of a hard shell and foam cushion to protect body parts against the impact of a fall. Now with easier-to-use boards, improved safety gear, and potential new tricks, skateboarding started to pick up again.

POWERSLIDE!

Coming into Style

Thanks to streamlined skateboards and new safety gear, people were discovering new ways to ride. To get the most from their boards, skaters took to riding down ramps and steep hills. This turned into something known as vertical skating—or **vert skating** for short. At the time, there were no skate parks for skaters to practice vert skating. Instead, many turned to (and sometimes even sneaked into) empty pools to skate along the smooth sides. Early icons of this style became famous for their amazing tricks.

One such icon was California skater Tony Alva. Born in Santa Monica, Alva grew up both surfing and skateboarding.

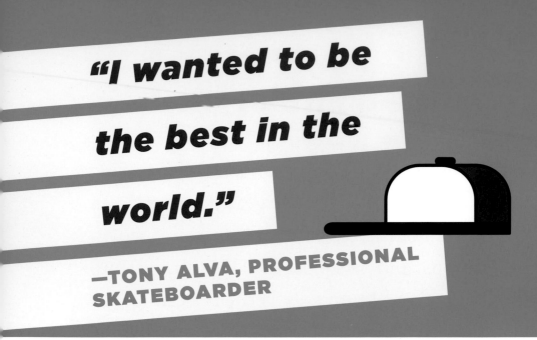

"I wanted to be the best in the world."

—TONY ALVA, PROFESSIONAL SKATEBOARDER

He soon became known for his fearless skateboarding, which he did in empty pools. In fact, Alva is often credited with being the first person to successfully land a frontside air—a move in which a skater rides up the side of a ramp (or pool) and then turns 180 degrees while in the air to ride back down the ramp. Thanks to his unique skating style and skill at landing new tricks, Alva is hailed as one of the pioneers of vert skating.

Skater Tony Alva shows off tricks for an audience.

A skateboarder does an ollie.

Other skaters were focusing on tricks, too. In the late 1970s, a skater named Alan "Ollie" Gelfand was credited with publicly debuting a new trick that would revolutionize skateboarding everywhere: the aptly named **ollie**. Now one of the most

The first person to successfully perform what is now called an "ollie" may have been a skater named Jeff Duerr— and the move was originally known as the "due air."

Skateboarding

How many styles of skateboarding are there? That depends on who you ask. Some of the best-known skateboarding styles are freestyle, vert, street, and park. However, some people categorize skateboarding into many other styles. Check out these skating styles:

Off-road

Freestyle: Freestyle skating involves skateboarding on flat ground—and sometimes making up moves, tricks, or choreography to music.

Vert: Vert skating usually involves riders skating down sloped surfaces to catch air and perform aerial tricks.

Street: Street skaters ride in urban or city environments. They use the objects around them—like handrails and street curbs—to perform tricks.

Park: Park skating, one of the most popular skateboarding styles today, involves riding and performing tricks at specially built skate parks.

Downhill: Downhill skaters seek sharp slopes where they can reach superfast speeds.

Off-road: Off-road skating? That's right! Also called mountainboarding, this style involves skateboarding down unpaved surfaces.

famous skateboarding tricks, an ollie is when a rider—and their skateboard—leap into the air without the rider using their hands. This new trick was tough—but it was also supercool. What's more, it now allowed riders to jump with their skateboards on or over other objects. And that led to an entirely new style of skating.

As the ollie caught on, people began using their boards to jump over objects or even slide along surfaces—also known as **grinding**. People also created new, more complex tricks using the ollie as their base. One such skater was Rodney Mullen, who invented numerous popular tricks, including the kickflip. The kickflip starts with an ollie, as the rider and board both leap into the air. Then, the rider causes the board itself to flip once around 180 degrees while in the air and lands perfectly back on the deck to continue riding. All together, these new tricks grew into a new style of skating: street skating. Skating had become its own sport—and was growing into a phenomenon.

A skater catches some air.

GNARLY!

"No one to this day has done ollies like [Gelfand] . . . He was . . . an originator."
—CRAIG SNYDER, AUTHOR

A Polish skater holds the record for the most skateboard ollies done in one minute: 82.

CHAPTER FIVE

Skate Culture

Skating for Everyone

As new skating styles developed, so did a skateboarding culture. At the forefront of that skating culture was an unspoken rule: Skateboarding pushed boundaries. Unlike many other sports, skating did not involve team activities or strict rules. It celebrated individuality, creativity, and breaking the rules—after all, it was a sport that prized making up new moves, developing unique personal styles, and even skating in places you weren't allowed to! These things helped turn it into a sport at the forefront of diversity and equality.

Throughout American sports history, many official sports organizations upheld racist views that prevented non-white

Venice Beach, California, became a center of skater culture.

people from joining. Although this began to slowly improve over the latter part of the twentieth century, people of color often still faced—and in many instances, continue to face today—unequal pay, underrepresentation, and racist treatment.

Many sports have also been exclusive in other ways. Some people can't join in on sports that require pricey gear or expensive club memberships. Other sports organizations have often excluded women from participating or have given women's sports teams fewer opportunities.

A **skater in** Venice Beach, California.

From its beginnings, skateboarding was a much more inclusive and diverse sport. Some of this had to do with the sport's birthplace: Southern California has long been a racially diverse place. Because of this, skateboarding was shaped by skaters who were Asian American, Latinx, Black, and more. On top of that, skaters came from many different financial backgrounds. Unlike many other sports, which require lessons or access to expensive equipment, skating could be done outside on the street or at a local park.

Perhaps most important, skateboarding was developing a reputation for breaking rules and pushing boundaries. In part, this was due to the skating pioneers—young people in their teens who were not afraid to shake up the status quo. In addition, skateboarding was a very new sport. That meant that the rules were always changing. In fact, there weren't any rules— people were making up the sport as they went. This made skateboarding a great fit for people who wanted to change the world in other ways.

"Skateboarders are envied by people because they just glide so free."

—MARK GONZALES, PROFESSIONAL SKATER

Of course, even skateboarding was not perfect—female skaters were often discouraged from skating, and people of color still faced the same systemic discrimination that occurred in much of their daily lives. But, thanks in part to the rebellious nature of skateboarding, many skaters pushed back against this discrimination and broke barriers in the skating community. In fact, many skaters who were people of color and women went on to define the skateboarding culture by creating their own skate companies and brands.

Tony Alva, a Mexican American skater and pioneer of vert skating, founded his own skating company in 1977 and went on to influence the sport for generations. Stacy Peralta, another icon of vert skating, had become the world's highest-ranked professional skater in 1976. Then, in 1984, he created the world's first skate video and became an indispensable part of skating culture.

Alva and Peralta were among the first skateboarding icons to push barriers, but they were far from the only ones. As a

Black female skater in the 1980s, Stephanie Person faced multiple barriers in the skateboarding world. But when she found that she didn't have as many opportunities as her male peers, Person refused to quit. Instead, she created and held her own skateboarding competition at just sixteen

"You were judged on your merit and how you could skate. You could stand up for what you believed was right, rather than being held down by what you looked like."

—MARTY GRIMES, PROFESSIONAL SKATER

Stephanie Person has competed in freestyle, street, and vert skating competitions.

years old. Person's event was a smash success: She had wrangled businesses and donors to give out prizes and attracted around five hundred participants. In fact, the event was such a hit that Person soon hosted another competition—and another after that! Soon, her skills caught sponsors' eyes, and she became the world's first professional Black female skater.

Today, more people than ever are skating—and are continuing to push back against racism and prejudice.

Skater Style

By the middle of the 1970s, skateboarding was back in full swing. Skateboarders were developing new styles, new moves, and their own culture. But that wasn't all—they were also creating a unique skateboarding style with its own fashion, music, and more.

Vans have a rubber sole designed to grip skateboard decks.

Starting in the 1960s, new clothing companies began to dedicate themselves to skate wear—especially skate shoes. In 1966, the Van Doren Rubber Company—known as Vans—debuted in Anaheim, California. The company quickly introduced a shoe designed to grip skateboard decks; the shoe was known as the deck shoe. Vans began to sponsor skaters around the country. Over the years, Vans became more and more known for its skate shoes as the company partnered with famous skaters like Alva and Peralta to introduce new designs.

Other companies introduced their own skate shoes over the years, including brands like Etnies and DC Shoes. Many skaters were also attracted to brands that catered to surfers—such as the Australian company Billabong or the California-based Quiksilver—but often paired their gear with other items that could withstand the more rough-and-tumble sport, such as jeans or baggy shorts.

As participants in an alternative sport, many skaters listened to alternative music. Whereas melodic, laid-back music had represented surfing, edgier rock and punk rock bands were favored by skaters. As the birthplace of skateboarding, California also lent the sport its sound with local nineties bands such as the Red Hot Chili Peppers, Green Day, The Offspring, Blink-182, and more. Their songs often featured long guitar

The crowd goes wild during the Vans Warped Tour. The skateboarding shoe company was the music festival's first sponsor.

"Skateboarding didn't wait for the world to change, we kind of changed that ourselves."

—CHUCK TREECE, PROFESSIONAL SKATEBOARDER

riffs, heavy drums, and fast-paced beats. Soon, some bands were even referencing skating in their lyrics, and others became famously known as "skate punk" bands.

However, one of the most important aspects of skater style was the skateboard itself. Early on, skaters took to decorating the undersides of their decks with custom art, known as deck art. To match the rebellious and individual nature of skateboarding, many people used graffiti-style art. Others incorporated surfing motifs like waves or art inspired by Native Pacific Islanders. Others still turned  to rock and punk rock styles for inspiration, decking out their decks with skulls or flames. Over time, deck artists became famous for their work, and decorated skateboards even became collectible items on their own.

Altogether, skateboarding had grown into a sort of counterculture—that is, an alternative to what mainstream culture views as popular or "normal." Skateboarding may have come from surfing, but by now it had evolved into a sport—and a cultural lifestyle—all its own.

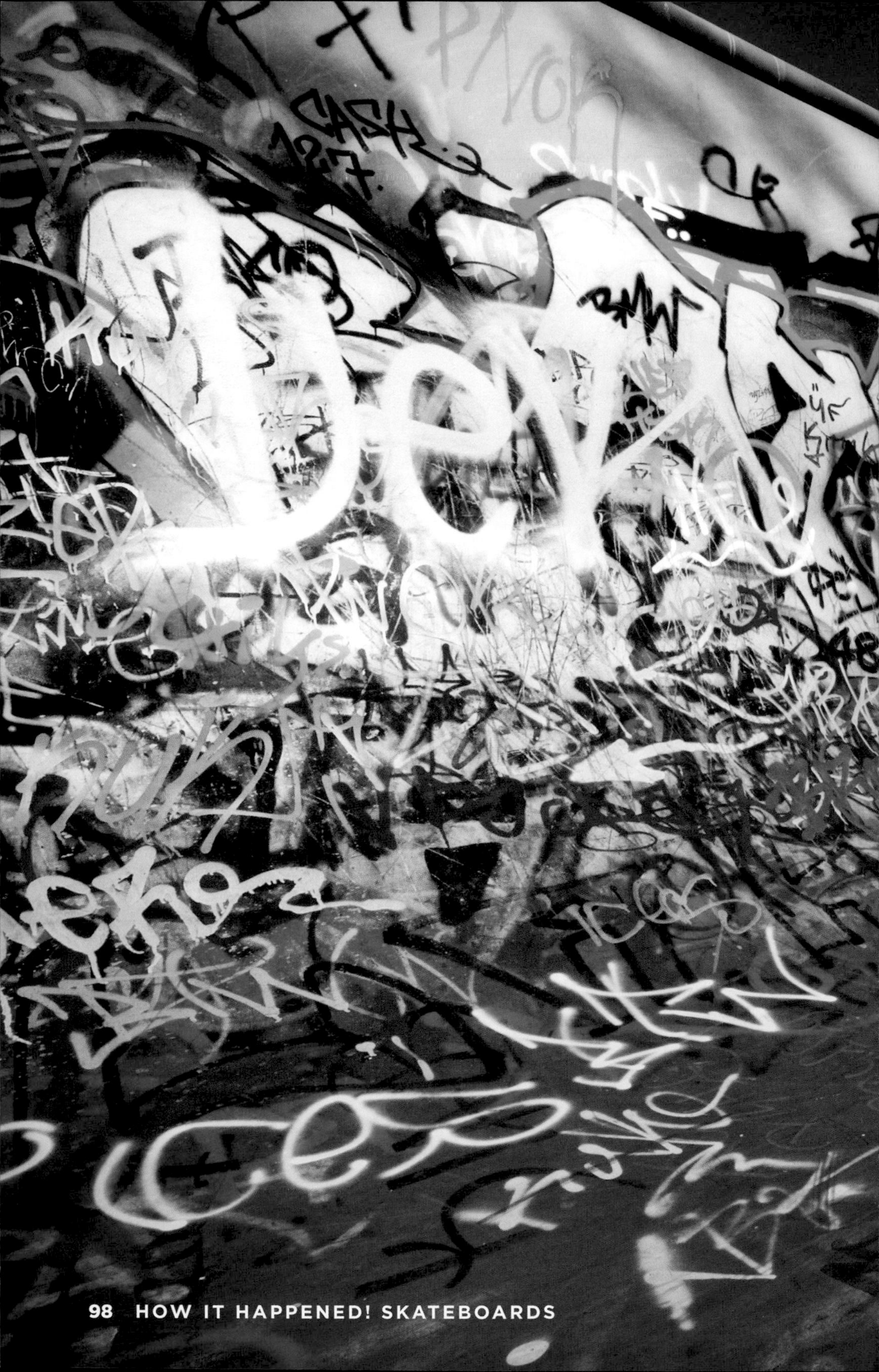

Great Graffiti

Graffiti has been around for thousands of years—in fact, archaeologists have found graffiti scrawled by ancient Romans, ancient Maya, Vikings, and more! But graffiti as an art style truly began to evolve in New York City in the 1970s. Street artists painted works onto public spaces (sometimes known as tagging). Some people viewed this as defacing public property. Others viewed graffiti as cutting-edge creative expression of counterculture. Today, many famous artists—such as Shepard Fairey, Jean-Michel Basquiat, and Banksy—are known for their street art. Like skateboarding, street artists chose to express themselves in public spaces with or without approval. This has made the sport and the art style a natural pairing!

Skater Style

Skateboarders had developed a rad counterculture with unique music and fashion, and skating icons of all different backgrounds were making history. But that didn't mean that things were smooth sailing—er, smooth skating that is!

For many people, skating was seen as a dangerous and rowdy sport. Injuries were more common than in other sports like soccer or baseball. But to many, skateboarding was more than dangerous—it was a nuisance.

Back in the 1970s, when skateboarding

was first gaining traction, there weren't many places for skaters to ride. Most skaters practiced freestyle and street skating and rode in the streets and other public places. This meant that the objects they were using—like public benches, rails, and other things—were sometimes getting damaged. On top of that, some skaters would even sneak into people's yards to skate in their empty pools!

Even when they were using skate parks, skaters weren't always welcome. For one thing, skateboarding can be loud. The sound of many wheels rolling and decks hitting the pavement often bothered people living or working near the park. Officials also worried about what would happen if skaters got injured while at the park.

This was especially true in places around the world where skateboarding was starting to take off. In Japan, when skateboarding

Decorated decks have been displayed in museums.

became popular in the 1970s, skaters were often looked down upon, and they were prevented from skating by police officers. "No Skateboarding" signs cropped up. In many towns and cities in Brazil, skateboarding was even banned. And in 1978, Norway banned skateboarding throughout the entire country.

On top of these concerns, skaters also faced unfair stereotypes and bad reputations. Because skating was known for individuality and not conforming, many people believed this meant skaters were reckless people—or even criminals. Of course, for most skaters, these stereotypes weren't at all true. Even so, in order for skateboarding to become viewed as a serious sport, many skaters would have to push back against these unfair views.

Hitting the Pool

In the 1970s, how did skaters in the United States luck out and find so many empty pools? After all, didn't people want to go swimming? As it happened, much of California was experiencing a terrible drought. During a drought, the weather remains unusually dry, with too little rain to keep crops healthy or provide water to local communities. While a drought is generally a bad thing for people and animals, it was lucky for skateboarders: To conserve water, many people chose to keep their pools empty. Because of this, empty pools were easy to find!

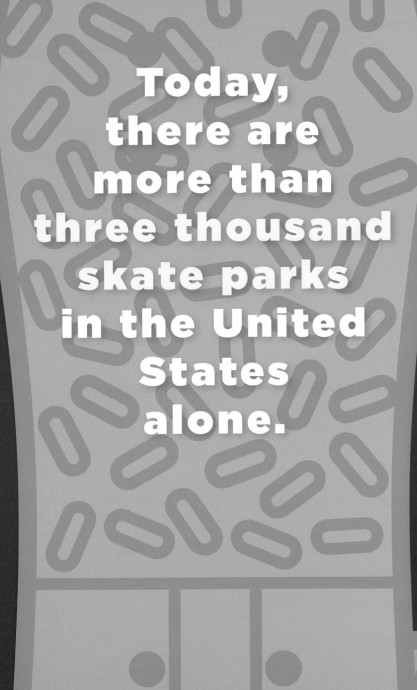

Today, there are more than three thousand skate parks in the United States alone.

CHAPTER SIX

The Competition Heats Up

Paving the Way

Ready to hit the **half-pipe**? Hold on— skateboarding wasn't there quite yet! People were gravitating to the sport and making it their own, but it was still widely considered an alternative hobby as opposed to a competitive sport.

When skateboarding first took off, competitions did start to appear. Makaha sponsored one of the first skateboarding contests in Hermosa Beach, California, in 1963. Soon, international competitions followed. But when safety concerns were raised about skateboards in the mid-1960s, these contests seemed to die out.

DOGTOWN AND Z-BOYS

Luckily, when inventors created better boards and safety gear in the 1970s, competitive skateboarders stepped up to the plate—er, stepped onto their boards.

One of the most influential competitive teams in skateboarding history was known as the Zephyr Competition Team— nicknamed the Z-Boys. Not surprisingly, the Z-Boys got their start in surfing, when a surfing company decided to found a surfing team, known as the Z-Boys, to represent

Tony Alva and the Z-Boys

their brand at competitions. However, a few years later, they pivoted to the new sport of skateboarding. By the mid-1970s, the Z-Boys consisted of twelve members, including skating legends such as Stacy Peralta, Tony Alva, Peggy Oki, Jay Adams, and others.

As new contests started to crop up, the Z-Boys blew away the competition. In 1975, they amazed audiences at the Bahne/Cadillac National Skateboard Championships with their takes on vert skating and the newly developing street style. The Z-Boys were known for their fluid, surf-like styles—and for crushing the competition. Many members earned high-ranking places—with Oki taking first place in the women's freestyle competition.

As the only woman of the Z-Boys, Oki broke new ground in the skateboarding

Welcome to Dogtown

As the Z-Boys rose in fame, so did one of the great birthplaces of skateboarding: Dogtown. Located in Southern California along Santa Monica, Dogtown was the name given to an abandoned area near a pier that had burned down in 1975. It was here that the Z-Boys often practiced skating along public places like sidewalks, parks, and schools. Today, the area is still known for its skating— but now it features official skate parks and boardwalks.

"Skateboarding is poetry of motion."

—STEVIE WILLIAMS, PROFESSIONAL SKATEBOARDER

An avid surfer and swimmer, Peggy Oki has since gone on to advocate for environmental awareness and ocean conservation.

world. As a result of outdated views on gender roles and the sport's rough nature, many people thought that skateboarding was inappropriate for girls. But Oki's skill, determination, and wins quickly debunked that myth. Altogether, the Z-Boys debunked another myth: that skateboarding was just a hobby.

Peggy Oki was a teenager when she joined the Z-Boys.

RAD!

With their numerous wins and obvious talent, the group demonstrated once and for all that skateboarding could be a competitive sport.

Making It Official

Thanks to skaters like the Z-Boys—along with the availability of safety equipment—skateboarding had become super popular by the start of the 1980s. For many people, it was now considered both an art and a sport. However, it hadn't yet hit the mainstream. In fact, skateboarding was still very much considered part of the counterculture. And it certainly wasn't recognized as a sport by official sports organizations! But that was starting to change.

Magazines aimed at skateboarders began to appear in the 1960s, but now more were hitting newsstands. In 1981, Californian

Rapper and producer Tyler, The Creator poses with a skateboard in Los Angeles, California.

Eric Swenson and Argentinian Fausto Vitello founded what would become a hugely influential magazine: *Thrasher*. The magazine included profiles of up-and-coming skaters and skateboard companies, as well as reviews of skate parks. *Transworld Skateboarding*, a rival magazine, was founded soon after in 1983. These magazines helped reach more and more people, pushing skateboarding into the mainstream spotlight.

There were also more places to skate than ever. One of the first skate parks had been built in 1976 in Florida. Now specially designated skate parks—as opposed to the streets and recreational parks—were popping up across the United States and Canada, as well as in Europe, Asia, and South America. Park skating—skateboarding done in a skate park as opposed to on the streets—started to become the sport's most popular style. On top of that, skaters were starting to attract **sponsorships** from skating companies. Brothers Clyde and Marty Grimes received EZ Ryder sponsorships in 1975, making them the first Black professional skaters.

Thanks to all of this attention, official organizations began to take a new look at the sport. In 1986, Canada hosted the Transworld Skateboard Championships. Germany's Münster Monster Mastership

Pro skater Jimmy Wilkins competes during the 2022 X Games held in Chiba, Japan.

was created in 1989, and World Cup Skateboarding was established in 1994.

Then, in 1993, the television network ESPN decided to host a competition dedicated to alternative sports—including skateboarding. Two years later, the first ever Extreme Games—now known as the X Games—were held across Rhode Island and Vermont. The games' sponsors were huge: Advil, Nike, Taco Bell, Mountain Dew, and more. And with 198,000 spectators in attendance, it's fair to say that these "alternative" sports like skateboarding weren't so alternative anymore.

Skateboarding was now an official competitive sport—and it had the events to prove it. By the mid-1990s, it was clear that skateboarding was here to stay.

Skater Slang

Over the years, skateboarders developed their own terminology and lingo. Check out some phrases here:

360: A move in which the skateboarder turns in a full circle.

ABD: This acronym—which stands for "already been done"—means that a move or trick has been mastered before.

A Bust: A spot that's not skateable for one reason or another.

Bowl: A skate bowl is the curved concrete or wooden structure often found in skate parks—or empty pools!

Face-plant: To fall off the board and onto the ground—face first!

Gnarly: A move or skating spot that is awesome—but also a little dangerous.

Goofy: Most riders naturally stand on their boards with their left foot forward. A stance where a rider places their right foot forward is known as goofy.

Half-pipe: The half-pipe is a ramp that curves up at both ends, allowing skaters to catch air for moves.

Rad: Something that is radical, or awesome.

Thanks to its curves, a half-pipe helps skaters gain speed and catch air.

How It Took Over the World

CHAPTER SEVEN

Exploding onto the Scene

Celebrity Skaters

So skateboarding was going mainstream, but it still needed to shed its rough reputation. The solution? Celebrity skaters. During the 1990s, skateboarders began to capture the public's attention in a new way. Now they were no longer just skate icons—they were becoming true celebrities in their own right.

Perhaps the best-known skater of all time is Tony Hawk. Born in 1968 in San Diego, California, Hawk went on to sweep most skateboarding competitions he entered. In addition to winning, Hawk became famous for his daredevil style, determination, and record-setting moves. In fact, in 1999, Hawk made history when he became the

Tony Hawk set new heights for skateboarding as a sport.

> ### "When I first started, skateboarding was so small you couldn't aspire to be rich and famous from it. You did it because you found something that spoke to you."
>
> **—TONY HAWK, PROFESSIONAL SKATEBOARDER**

first person to successfully land a 900: a two-and-a-half vertical rotation off a vertical ramp.

And Tony Hawk is far from the only skateboarder to emerge as a celebrity. Born in 1968 in South Gate, California, Mark Gonzales was both an early icon of skating

and a skate artist—someone known for creating amazing deck art. He often appeared in magazines such as *Thrasher* and put San Francisco's neighborhoods on the skating scene. However, on top of being an influential "founding father" of skateboarding, Gonzales also became a

Mark Gonzales performs a trick called an invert in Orange County, California.

celebrity in the 1990s when he began appearing in music videos, partnering with famous brands to design skate gear, working as a director, and showing his art in exhibitions.

Thanks to these celebrity skaters, public opinion of skateboarding began to change. Of course, it was still cool and creative—but now the public was seeing that skateboarders were also inspiring role models, business owners, artists, activists, and more.

Skating Around the World

Although the birthplace of skateboarding was the United States, skating quickly spread to other countries and continents. In the 1970s, young skaters in the United

Kingdom began to import their own boards from American skateboard manufacturers. However, health and safety experts in Britain quickly warned against the sport, saying that it could cause serious injuries. Because of this, skateboarding in the U.K. slowed for several years but quickly took off again once the sport hit the mainstream in the 1990s.

Meanwhile, skateboarding had also arrived in another European country: Germany. In the middle of the twentieth

China's GMP Skatepark is the largest skate park in the world. It's the size of around thirteen Olympic swimming pools.

Roll Along

As skateboards spread around the world, so did different styles of boards—including longboards. Like a skateboard, a longboard is made up of a deck on four wheels. However, longboards are much, well, longer, and they tend to be wider. This makes them easier to balance on and perfect for using as transportation. It can be tricky to perform traditional skateboard moves on longboards, but the distinct boards are often used for other types of competitions, such as downhill racing.

century, the United States
had kept American soldiers
stationed in parts of what is now Germany.
This was in part because of World War II, an
enormous war that involved more than
thirty countries and lasted from 1939 to
1945. After the war's end, American troops
continued to occupy parts of Europe
because of a rivalry that developed with
the Soviet Union, a republic made up of
fifteen modern countries including Russia
and many Eastern European countries.
To prevent the Soviet Union from gaining
more power, the United States continued
to maintain troops in countries such as
Germany. This had an unintended outcome:
American soldiers began to bring
their skateboards with them.
Because of this, skateboarding
took off in Germany.

In one move, Bob Burnquist skated out of a helicopter and onto a ramp.

Perhaps unsurprisingly, skateboarding spread to countries where surfing was popular—such as Australia, Brazil, and South Africa. As in the U.K., skateboarding received a chilly welcome in Brazil. But Brazilian skaters refused to quit: In 1978, the first Brazilian skater magazine, *Brasil Skate*, was published. The same year, a skate park was built in Rio de Janeiro.

In fact, Brazilian riders soon developed a new skateboarding style known as Brazilian style. The style often features fast skating, fluid movements, and many aerial moves. One Brazilian skater in particular, Bob Burnquist, elevated his incredible skating career from that of skateboard icon to international celebrity. On top of winning many championships, Burnquist became famous for his death-defying skateboard stunts, and he went on to appear on TV

Girls in Afghanistan practice their skateboarding.

shows, voice act in cartoons, and even work as an environmental activist. Brazil remains a top destination for skaters, and in 2019, it hosted the World Park Skateboarding Championships.

Skateboarding was also a natural fit in South Africa, where surfers had been catching waves for decades. However, the sport also gained momentum in its own right and soon spread to places where surfing hadn't been as popular. Thanks to skating

videos, street skateboarding was on the rise in Kenya by the 2000s. Skateboarding also took off in other countries across the continent, including Uganda, Rwanda, Ethiopia, Ghana, and more.

Just like in skateboarding's birthplace, California, skating in these countries was at first done only on the streets. But thanks to the sport's can-do, counterculture mindset, skaters have been pushing boundaries and building skate parks. In fact, the skating culture in these countries has taken on its own unique style and character. Here, skateboarding has become a sport of both counterculture and community. In 2013, enterprising skateboarders came together to create a skate park in Nairobi. Today, Shangilia Skate Park is the largest skate part in eastern Africa. In Ethiopia, a grassroots group of skaters helped open the country's

China's skateboarding scene is among the world's largest.

first skate park in 2016. And in Ghana, a skate park that opened in 2021 also inspired the creation of an all-women skateboarding group known as Skate Gal Club.

Where will skateboarding go next? It's hard to say. But it's clear that wherever it goes, the sport remains a driver for innovation, creativity, and personal expression.

Tough Tricks

Before Tony Hawk landed the world's first 900, people weren't sure it was possible. In fact, only a few skaters have successfully landed the move since Hawk first accomplished it. But in 2021, twenty-two years after Hawk landed the 900, another skater took it even further. At just twelve years old, Brazilian Gui Khury successfully landed a 1080 in a competition: a full *three* vertical rotations off a vertical ramp!

022 Pr

CHAPTER EIGHT

Skating in Pop Culture

Hitting the Screens

From its start, skateboarding had been linked to videos. Many skaters often filmed their moves and shared the videos with each other or with sponsors. But over time, the relationship between skateboarding and film grew. In 2001, a documentary featuring the rise of skateboarding called *Dogtown and Z-Boys* premiered at the Sundance Film Festival. The film was a smash hit and went on to win more than ten awards. In 2005, the documentary was even made into a fictional movie, *Lords of Dogtown,* starring the actor Heath Ledger. Other companies made their own documentaries, too, such as *Pretty Sweet* or Transworld Skateboarding's *Duets.*

Actor Emile Hirsch plays a skater in a scene from the movie *Lords of Dogtown.*

Marty McFly, played by actor Michael J. Fox, rides a skateboard in a scene from *Back to the Future.*

Girl: "What's that thing he's riding?"

Guy: "It's a board with wheels!"

—*BACK TO THE FUTURE*, A FILM IN WHICH A KID LIVING IN THE 1980S TRAVELS BACK TO 1955

Documentaries and movies weren't the only ways skateboarding made it to the screen. TV shows started to feature skateboarders, too. Among the first skateboarding characters was the iconic Bart Simpson of *The Simpsons*. Matching skateboarder stereotypes, the show debuted in 1989 with Bart as a back-talking, rebellious skater who enjoyed skating on public property. (And in one episode, Bart even got to meet skateboarding legend Tony Hawk, who actually voiced the animated version of himself.) But Bart was far from the last skateboarder; other shows highlighting skateboarders included Disney's *Zeke and Luther*, and Netflix's *Stranger Things* and *Arcane: League of Legends*.

Skateboarding also became popular with the actors themselves. In fact, actors, musicians, and other celebrities—such as

There are now more than twenty games in the *Tony Hawk Pro Skater* series.

Miley Cyrus; Chloë Moretz; Selena Gomez; Rich the Kid; Tyler, The Creator; and many more—were often spotted riding or carrying boards.

And skateboarding broke onto the silver screen in other ways, too. In fact, the most influential skating on screen wasn't a show or movie at all. In 1999, Activision released the video game *Tony Hawk's Pro Skater*. The game quickly became one of the most popular video game series of the next decade, making fans out of both people who skated and those who never had. In fact, the game was so popular that it raised skateboarding to new heights—and spawned many new skateboarding video games, including more in the *Tony Hawk* series and other games such as *Skate, Shaun White Skateboarding,* and *OlliOlli.*

GROOVY!

Beyond Skating

Far from its days as part of the counterculture, skateboarding seemed to be taking over the world. In fact, it was now influencing areas completely *outside* of skateboarding.

Starting in the 1960s, American toy companies began to make miniature skateboards meant to be "ridden" with a person's fingers. This new game, known as fingerboarding, took off over the years. Kids

Some people can perform complicated skateboard tricks—like the 360—with fingerboards.

would use two fingers like legs to "ride" the mini boards over tables and other smooth surfaces—and even perform moves like ollies! And after the Canadian toy company Tech Deck launched a new fingerboarding line in the 1990s, these miniature boards even became collectibles. Some were even marked with the logos and designs of real skateboard companies.

In addition to toys, skateboarding was continuing to influence fashions. However, while skater styles were mostly popular with alternative crowds or as relaxed, everyday wear, fashion houses were starting to take notice too. Soon, designer labels such as DKNY, Louis Vuitton, Gucci, and more began to take inspiration from skateboarder styles, creating expensive versions of hoodies, baggy pants, and even footwear inspired by skateboarding shoes.

A few brands even began to feature famous skaters such as Dylan Rieder and Blondey McCoy in their ads or send models down runways on skateboards! What's more, some skate brands—from Supreme to Stüssy to Palace—soon earned the status of high fashion themselves.

Similarly, in the early 2000s, the skate-inspired punk rock and skate punk music styles continued to evolve in new ways, with the emergence of artists such as Canadian singer Avril Lavigne and styles such as pop punk. Pop punk artists merged the gritty, fast-paced tempos and electric guitar riffs of earlier punk rock styles with the more mainstream melodies of pop.

In fact, skateboarding's influence on music and fashion can still be seen today in the resurgence of early 2000s fashion and music! Pop punk has experienced a revival

Music artist Avril Lavigne poses with a skateboard on the Hollywood Walk of Fame.

as its gritty-meets-mainstream sounds have graced the albums of artists such as Lil Nas X and Olivia Rodrigo. Similarly, popular fashion has seen a return to casual, comfy skater clothes such as sweatpant and sweatshirt sets, fashionable beanies, and wide-leg jeans.

Now, far from having a bad reputation or being seen as an outsider's sport, skateboarding influences television, toys, fashion, music, and more.

The Dog Days of Skateboarding

As skateboarding became a worldwide phenomenon, more and more people joined in—and so did some animals! The most famous of these may have been Tillman, the skateboarding English bulldog. Known for his love of—and skill at—skateboarding, Tillman held a world record for fastest dog on a skateboard.

CHAPTER NINE

Changing the Rules

New to the Scene

Skateboarding had hit the big leagues. But now it was time to conquer the biggest league of them all: the Olympics.

After the 2016 Olympics, officials were interested in attracting more younger viewers and competitors. The next Summer Olympics would be held in Tokyo in 2020, and they wanted to add something fresh and new. They had an idea: What about skateboarding? After all, its popularity was at an all-time high. Thousands of people had even been petitioning for the sport to be added. But many people were also against it—and, surprisingly, some of them were skateboarders.

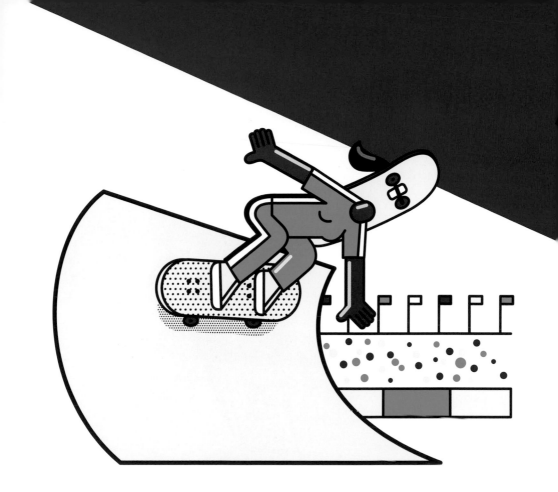

Many skateboarders worried that adding their sport to the Olympics would take away part of what makes the sport special. Would people still be able to innovate and use skateboarding as personal expression? Would the rules and points scoring system be too rigid and discourage creativity? For some people, adding skateboarding to the

Olympics would represent a final seal of approval, proving that skateboarding is an official, competitive sport. To others, the decision didn't represent the rebellious heart of the sport.

Despite the fears, skateboarding debuted as an Olympic sport at the 2020 Tokyo Summer Olympics. The competitions were split into two styles: park, which included a choreographed skate run, and street, for which competitors attempted to land complicated and difficult moves. Japanese pro skateboarder Yuto Horigome made history when he won gold in the men's street category, becoming the first ever skateboarder to win gold at the Olympics.

So was the event a success? That depends on who you ask—and that's what makes skateboarding special! Some people think that skateboarding is better as a personal hobby, an art form, or a countercultural sport. To others, the Olympics was an inspiring look at some

Momiji Nishiya at the women's street competition at the 2020 Olympics.

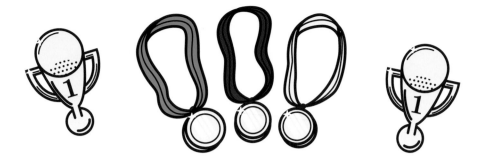

of the world's top young skaters who are taking the sport in new directions. In fact, skateboarders represented many of the youngest competitors at the Olympics—such as Japanese skater Momiji Nishiya, who won the gold in women's street at just thirteen years old. To some skaters, this represents a whole new future of skateboarding, and it proves that young people around the world will continue skating and taking it to new heights.

Regardless of whether a person prefers to skate for themselves, skate competitively, or even skate at the Olympics, one thing is clear: Skateboarding has officially taken over the world. Not only that, but it will continue to change and grow.

Changing the Game

Thanks to social media—and thanks to the many skateboarders who paved the way—skateboarding has opened up to more people than ever. In fact, social media helps people of all different backgrounds get sponsors or become famous skaters. As long as they have the skill, it doesn't matter what their race, gender, or background is.

Now, people are using skateboarding to make even more social changes. Across the world, many athletes are using skateboarding to create welcoming and safe spaces for LGBTQIA+ skaters. One such organization is the nonprofit Black Girls Skate (BGS). Founded in 2019, BGS tours the United States to promote equality for skaters who identify as LGBTQIA+ through education and pop-ups. The group aims to provide safe places for skaters to ride.

Sky Brown

Nyjah Huston

Game Changers

Since the early 2000s, skateboarders have continued to redefine skateboarding. Check out some skating superstars from the past few years:

Sky Brown: At just fourteen, Brown was described by Tony Hawk as "one of the best well-rounded skaters ever." The British Japanese international skateboarding icon is known for her fearless skating, as well as being an author and social media star.

Nyjah Huston: A six-time skateboarding World Champion and thirteen-time X Games gold medalist, Huston is an American skater famed for his signature move, the Nyjah frontside air.

Letícia Bufoni: A six-time X Games gold medalist, the Brazilian skater has appeared in the Guinness World Records for the most World Cup Skateboarding wins.

Letícia Bufoni

Super Skateboarding

When it comes to sports, it's true that skateboarding can be on the rougher side—after all, it involves falling a lot. But skateboarding has lots of benefits, too! People who skateboard improve their strength, cardio health, and coordination. According to experts, skateboarding can also lower stress and improve patience. And skate parks provide social opportunities to young people across the world and can even help reduce crime among young people by providing places to gather and hang out, as well as an outlet for self-expression.

Members and friends of Black Girls Skate hang out in New York City. The group's goal is to promote inclusion in skateboarding.

Skateboarding can also help to promote activism, inclusion, and equal rights for many other people around the world. In Bolivia, the all-women skate group ImillaSkate raises awareness for both Indigenous communities in Bolivia and women's rights. In fact, the women often skate in traditional outfits known as *polleras* to honor their heritage, fight against discrimination, and draw attention

"*Skateboarding influenced my life a lot; it filled me with courage when I needed it most. And it is something that I would like to be able to share with other people.*"

—HUARA MEDINA MONTAÑO, IMILLASKATE MEMBER

to the historical persecution of Aymara and Quechua populations in Bolivia.

Similarly, Diné skateboarder Naiomi Glasses uses her presence on social media to promote her Diné (Navajo) heritage and to help bring skate parks to reservations across the United States. Other groups

and companies in the country—such as Colonialism Skateboards and Nations Skate Youth—also promote equal opportunities and representation for Indigenous youth and skateboarders. And in Australia, Songline Skateboarding has become the first all-Aboriginal skateboarding team.

It is clear that not only has skateboarding already changed the world—from fashion to sports to music and more—but it will continue to do so.

A member of ImillaSkate at a park in La Paz, Bolivia.

Going Big

In 2004, the X Games debuted a new skating structure: the mega ramp. Like the half-pipe, the mega ramp was a steep structure that let skateboarders catch air to land complicated moves. However, the mega ramp was much taller, much steeper, and much more dangerous. This risky skating style also gave way to new daredevil stunts, as well as a new skating style known as big air. In 2006, legendary skater Bob Burnquist used a ramp to skateboard out over the Grand Canyon, where he then deployed a parachute to land safely!

Bob Burnquist
has his own
private skate
park, known
as Dreamland,
which includes
a mega ramp.

Skating into the Future

CHAPTER TEN

Redefining Skateboarding

What's Next for Skaters?

With such amazing culture, style, tricks, and more, is there really much left for the future of skateboarding? Absolutely! After all, innovation is one of the most important aspects of the sport.

Already, scientists and other innovators are experimenting with ways to take skateboarding to the next level. Google's Project Skate uses machine learning, a type of artificial intelligence, to track skaters' stats such as speed, rotations, height, and more. This lets skaters analyze their performances with real mathematical data to help themselves improve or spot weaknesses. On top of that, there are

Virtual skateboarding is on the rise.

companies looking to popularize electronic skateboards that rely on batteries instead of push power. Some companies are instead aiming to develop better trucks, decks, and wheels that let skaters achieve new heights. And others are focusing on virtual skateboarding: skateboarding that takes place in virtual reality and doesn't involve a physical board at all.

More important, other innovators are developing ways that expand *who* can skate. To make skateboarding even more inclusive, some are crafting prototypes of devices that let people in wheelchairs or with other mobility concerns join in. One such device, created by a wheelchair user named Erik Kondo, lets a wheelchair rest on top of a motorized skateboard that responds to the rider's balance. Other adaptive skateboarders prefer to use streamlined wheelchairs as the skateboards themselves and use the chairs to perform moves at skate parks or on ramps. People still are working toward including skateboarding in the 2028 Paralympics, and they hope that the inclusion of adaptive skateboarding will inspire more companies and engineers to create alternative skateboards.

No matter how skateboarding changes, one thing is for sure: innovation will always be a part of skateboarding.

"Wheelchair motocross" or WCMX, world champion Lily Rice was the first woman in the United Kingdom to complete a backflip in a wheelchair.

A Tricked-Out Timeline

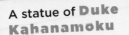
A statue of **Duke Kahanamoku**

circa 2000 BCE

People in what is now Peru surf on *caballitos de totora.*

circa 1500 BCE

The Lapita people set out to explore and settle what will be known as the Pacific.

circa 1400

The oldest-known record of surfing is carved in a petroglyph in Tonga.

1890

Duke Kahanamoku is born and goes on to popularize surfing in the United States, Australia, and elsewhere.

1950s

Innovators create some of the first sidewalk surfboards.

1960s

Freestyle skateboarding appears.

1965

Patti McGee lands on the cover of *Life* magazine doing a handstand on her skateboard.

Longboard wheels

1969	1970s	1973
Larry Stevenson invents the kicktail.	The ollie is invented, and street skating becomes popular.	Frank Nasworthy invents the polyurethane wheel.

1990s

Punk rock and skate punk become popular.

1994

World Cup Skateboarding is established.

1995

The first X Games (formerly known as Extreme Games) are held.

1999

Tony Hawk
becomes the first
person to land a
900.

1999

*Tony Hawk's Pro
Skater* is released.

Momiji Nishiya competes during the 2020 Olympics held in Tokyo, Japan.

2001

The smash-hit documentary *Dogtown and Z-Boys* premieres at the Sundance Film Festival.

2004

The mega ramp is debuted at the X Games.

2021

Yuto Horigome becomes the first ever person to win an Olympic gold in skateboarding.

2021

Momiji Nishiya becomes one of the three youngest people to win a gold medal at the Olympics when she places first in women's street skateboarding.

2021

Gui Khury lands a 1080 on a vert ramp during the X Games.

2023

Thirteen-year-old Arisa Trew becomes the first female skater to land a 720.

Time to Innovate!

The super-rad story of the skateboard is one of creativity, perseverance, and boundary-breaking innovation. Get your own innovation in gear with these skateboard-inspired activities.

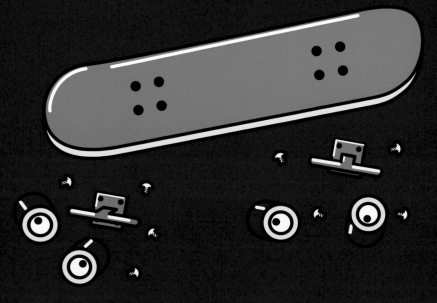

Make Your Move

Skateboarders are always trying to take things further and reach new heights. Try researching existing skateboarding moves and then come up with a brand-new move that you think would be totally rad. What kind of skating style would your move belong to?

Design a Deck Graphic

Deck graphics are a way for skateboarders to customize their boards and express themselves creatively. Deck graphics have even been displayed in museums! Design and draw a graphic that expresses who you are.

Change the Game

Skateboarding got its start when surfers wanted to find new ways to ride. Think about some existing sports. Can you create a new sport inspired by one that already exists? What would you call the new sport?

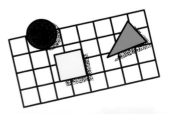

Glossary

Aerial: Movements or tricks done in the air

Axle: The fixed rod or bar between a pair of wheels that allows for rotation

Buoyancy: The upward force a fluid places on an object

Counterculture: A lifestyle or style that is different from what is viewed as "popular" or "normal"

Deck: The board of a skateboard

Drought: A period of unusually dry weather with little or no rainfall

Freestyle: A style of skateboarding that is done on flat ground, often to music

Friction: A resistant force

Gravity: The downward pull one object exerts on another

Grinding: Sliding along a surface using a skateboard

Grip tape: The rough, slightly sticky material that covers the deck of a skateboard

Half-pipe: A curved structure for skateboarding that allows riders to catch air

Hydrodynamics: The study of fluids in motion

Kicktail: The upward-curved end of the skateboard

Momentum: The force or moving weight of an object in motion

Nose: The front of a skateboard

Ollie: A skateboarding trick in which a rider leaps with their skateboard into the air without using their hands

Petroglyph: A rock carving

Polyurethane: A flexible material often used to make skateboard wheels

Sponsorship: Financial support from a sponsor, often a company

Tail: The back of a skateboard

Territory: An area of land ruled by a country or organization but not formally incorporated

Truck: The devices that allow a rider to steer the skateboard

Vert skating: A style of skateboarding in which skaters ride their boards on ramps or half-pipes

Wayfinder: The name for a person navigating through wilderness, often used for ancient explorers of the Pacific

Note: Some of these words may have more than one meaning. These definitions match what the words mean in this book.

Index